EXAMPLES OF FINE WILLOW WORK.

Covered Bottle, French.
Wine Basket, French.
Key Basket in Skein Work, English.
Pool Basket, French.
Work Basket in Flat Skein Work, English.
Key Basket, French

WILLOW
BASKET-WORK

A. G. KNOCK

Arthur Pearson Prize Winner, College of Teachers of the Blind ;
Prize Winner, City and Guilds of London Institute

THE DRYAD PRESS
LEICESTER

FOURTH EDITION 1951

PUBLISHED BY THE DRYAD PRESS AND PRINTED IN GREAT BRITAIN BY
HAZELL WATSON & VINEY, LTD., AYLESBURY AND LONDON

CONTENTS

	Page
ͻ	7
L AND EQUIPMENT	9
ICAL TERMS	14
ODS OF WEAVING	16
ERS AND HANDLES	22
IN WORK	30
UND WORK	38
OVAL WORK	45
RECTANGULAR WORK	49
OTHER SHAPES AND KINDS OF WORK . . .	54

3

LIST OF ILLUSTRATIONS

MPLES OF FINE WILLOW WORK . . *Frontispiece*

              Facing page

ORRECT POSITIONS FOR WORKING . . . 14

ROUND WHITE BREAD OR FRUIT BASKET, CLOSE-
RANDED BUFF PICNIC BASKET 15

BOAT BASKET, LIDDED " SOUTHPORT " BASKET, OBLONG
BUFF BABY'S OR WORK BASKET 42

. ROUND BUFF SHOPPING BASKET, HALF-MOON BUFF
CYCLE BASKET 43

5. ROUND BROWN-AND-WHITE BLACKBERRY BASKET, OVAL
BROWN-AND-WHITE GARDEN BASKET, OVAL BUFF
SHOPPING BASKET, WILLOW-EDGED TRAY . . 50

FOREWORD

THIS text book deals with the class of willow basket-work known in the workshop by the old, but now somewhat misleading, name of "fancy work," to distinguish it from the larger and coarser kinds and those that are strictly utilitarian. The author puts forward "fine" as a better adjective, suggesting as it does not only the above meaning, but also the attempt to achieve elegance, beauty, perfection.

The primitive and universal art of basket-work is essentially handicraft, and as such is of educational and curative value, and can be taken up with only a small initial outlay in tools and material. The instructions given here are based on traditional British technique, which is capable of producing a wide variety of pattern and an infinite number of shapes, when, after mastering the conventional forms exemplified here, the worker gives rein to his fancy. But it is important that, after some mastery over the material is gained, the novice should endeavour to work strictly to a shape and measurements previously determined upon. Nothing is easier than to allow the work to get out of hand, and if this happens the only real remedy is the drastic one of taking it back and doing it again.

Broadly speaking, round-shaped work is the simplest, oval coming next, and then square-cornered work. Wooden bottoms or bases are of material assistance in the earlier attempts, but it is more craftsmanlike, except in the case of trays, to make the article of willow throughout if the shape is a fairly simple one. In the case of out-of-the-ordinary shapes, however, wooden bottoms are recommended.

The exterior decoration of baskets by spraying, dyeing, or brush painting will appeal to some; others will prefer the natural beauty of the willow unadorned, except perhaps for a coat of clear varnish.

Unfortunately, willow basket-work is not a craft that can be easily explained in a book; but the writer has done his best within the space available, and hopes that this effort will at least prove a useful complement to personal instruction.

MATERIAL AND EQUIPMENT

MATERIAL.—Of the materials for fine willow basket-work, that almost exclusively used is naturally the willow, more specifically the cultivated Basket Willow, Osier, or Withy, from which one-year-old shoots are cut, these being known in the trade as Rods. The best rods are those which have finely tapered tops; good length in proportion to thickness; freedom from side shoots, "scabs," "bubbles," and other blemishes; good colour; relative smallness of pith; and maximum pliability.

The grower prepares rods in three ways : by peeling, which produces White; by peeling after boiling, which results in Buff; and as Brown, the trade name for rods dried with the peel on, whatever its colour. Rods are bought by length, not thickness, as in the case of cane. For fine work the trade lengths, which approximate to the average length of the rods in the bundle, are as follows, the old trade names, still sometimes used, being given also: Three feet, Tacks; four feet, Short-Small; five feet, Long-Small; six feet, Threepenny. Very small rods, such as the variety known as Dicky Meadows, are sorted into four or five lengths, the shortest consisting of rods up to eighteen inches. The material is sold by weight, or by the Bundle, Bunch or Bolt, of standard girth, the weight of a bundle varying according to its length.

Willows must be stored in a dry place or they will become mildewed. For the same reason any soaked material left over should be thoroughly dried before being put away. Soaking under water is necessary to render willows pliable enough to be worked. Brown rods should be left under water for two or three days, and then lie under a piece of damp sacking or cloth for another day to mellow. White and buff rods require from fifteen minutes, for the Dicky-Meadow type of rods, to an all-night soak for the six-foot variety.

It is not possible to give hard-and-fast times for soaking,

9

as different crops of willows, coming from different parts, each crop having experienced different growing conditions, tend to vary in the pith content. Usually the more pithy the content, the less time required for soaking. Argentine and African willows have very little core, and require more soaking than the English willow of the same size, but they are very good willows when conditioned for working.

Buff willows as a rule do not require quite so much soaking as white.

Having soaked the rods for the required time, they should be lifted out of the tank and stood on their butts to drain for half an hour out of wind and sun. This draining takes place internally as well as externally, allowing the water to drain down the pithy core into the thicker butt where it is most required. The rods should then be laid down out of any draught and covered with sacking, which has been thoroughly soaked in water and wrung out again so that it is scarcely damp all over.

Very wet sacking should not be used as it does not allow rods to dry off on their outsides. Willows in condition should feel just damp and velvety to the touch, with no trace of greasiness.

Time for leaving under the sacking before working will vary from one to five or six hours according to size, and the factors mentioned in connection with soaking govern this also. The feel of the rods is the best way to judge. Are they ready for working or not?

The greasiness referred to can be brought about by leaving rods too long under sacking before they are worked up. Heating takes place in the bundle of willows, which sweat, causing greasiness, and it is quite impossible to work them in this state. If this does happen, or some mildew shows in the bundle, wash each willow rod, running the hand up each one. Stand on the butts to drain and cover them down again. Then work them up as soon as all the water has disappeared from the outside of the willows.

It is best to condition the amount which can be worked up in two days. At all times work from the willows under the sacking. Do not uncover them, and at all times avoid draughts and sun.

Equipment.—Willow work cannot be done in an ordinary

living-room without causing inconvenience to other occupants and "making a mess." It is therefore desirable to have a space somewhere set apart for the purpose. In the trade, basket-makers work on the floor or on an oblong "plank" raised a few inches above it, with a low box at one end against the wall for use as a seat in much of the work. For fine work, however, a table and chair can be used, with the covered rods lying on the floor, except for the few needed for immediate use, which can lie on the table.

Tank.—Small quantities of rods can be soaked in a bath if something heavy is placed on them to keep them under water, or in a rain-water tank if reasonably clean. But the best method is to use an oblong galvanised tank, say about four feet or five feet long by about one foot or one foot six inches in width and depth, with an inside flange under which lengths of wood fit across the tank to keep the rods under water.

Work-Board.—Two forms are shown on Plate 1. That at the bottom will probably be preferred for small baskets, but in the case of deeper ones such as linen baskets, it is not possible to remain seated at the table, as the work gets so high as to be out of reach. One must then either stand or use the board shown in the upper part of the illustration, with its nearer end lowered and resting on a stool or other support. It should be noted that baskets with sloping sides should not stand horizontally when being worked, but should tilt away from worker as shown.

Screw-Block.—This is used for holding the sticks when bottoms and lids of rectangular work are being made (see illustration).

Hand-Knife.—So called to distinguish it from the Picking-Knife (see illustration). The blade should be sharp right up to the ferrule.

Picking-Knife.—This is a special tool of the shape illustrated, used for cutting off surplus ends from the work. The blade is sharpened only along the end, pressure downwards severing the piece to be cut off.

Sharpening Stone.—Both the above-mentioned knives must be kept absolutely sharp, for which purpose either a Whetstone, Oilstone, or Shoemaker's Buff may be used.

Shears.—These are similar to a gardener's pruning

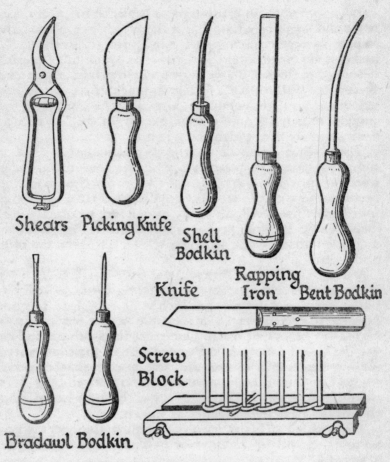

Shears   Picking Knife

Shell Bodkin

Knife   Rapping Iron   Bent Bodkin

Screw Block

Bradawl Bodkin

shears, and those illustrated are ideal for fine basket work. Shears having the spring extending along the inside of one handle should be avoided. Sharpening is necessary only at long intervals. An occasional drop of oil where the two halves meet makes for easy working.

Bodkins.—These, as will be seen from the illustration, are not the bodkins used in needlework. Three kinds are shown. The Shell Bodkin, pushed through the work, facilitates the passing through of a rod, the end of which is pushed along the hollow of the bodkin blade, which is then withdrawn. The Bent Bodkin is handy for inserting handle-bows in a basket with curved sides. The ordinary Bodkin, which is made in several sizes, is used in "staking up," "cramming off," and in all cases where a rod has to be pushed into or through the work. To avoid repetition the use of the bodkin is not referred to in the instructions, but it should be understood that the bodkin is in frequent use, and is a great saver of time and patience. For greasing the bodkin so that it enters the work easily, Russian tallow or similar grease is used. This can be kept in a tube such as a piece of gas piping about half an inch in diameter and four or five inches long, closed at one end. The bodkin is thrust into the open end before use.

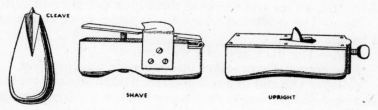

Rapping Iron.—That illustrated is suitable for the finest work, but one somewhat heavier will be more appropriate for larger baskets. Its chief function is to close down the work, and it is also used for any other purpose where hammer-like blows are required.

Cleave, Shave, and Upright.—These are used for making skeins, as explained in the section "Skein Work."

Rule or Measure-Stick.—An ordinary non-folding carpenter's rule is suitable. This can be two feet long or three feet if the size of the work necessitates, and should be plainly marked in inches subdivided into eighths.

Bradawl.—This is used for pinning work to board, and one with a long thin blade, as illustrated, is best. A weight of some kind can also be used, either with or without the awl.

A useful addition to the tool-kit is a pair of pincers for withdrawing rods which cannot be gripped by the fingers.

TECHNICAL TERMS

TECHNICAL terms are tiresome perhaps, but can hardly be dispensed with. The following, with minor modifications, are those used in the trade and have been reduced to the minimum necessary for the work we are attempting:

Border.—The piece of work which neatly finishes off the sides, lid, or foot of a basket. It is formed by bringing down the stakes and working them into a definite pattern.

Bow.—The stout rod which forms the core or centre of a handle.

Butt.—The thick end of a willow rod.

Bye-Stakes.—Extra stakes inserted after the upsetting.

Cram.—The end of a rod pointed, turned at right angles, and pushed into the work. Mainly used in finishing a plain border.

Fitch.—A pair of rods worked in the reverse way to pairing, and used to form open-work.

Flow.—The outward slope of the sides of a basket.

Foot.—A piece of work consisting of one or more rounds of waling and a border, added to the bottom of a basket.

Front.—Where this term is used in the instructions it means that side of the work which faces worker.

Handle.—The main kinds of basket handle are the Cross Handle and the Small Handle, the latter being either on the border or below it.

Hinge.—Formed of twisted rod or skein, and used to attach a lid to a basket.

Hoop.—Formed by coiling a rod upon itself, and used to keep stakes upright until upsett has been worked. Also applied to the rigid framework used in "Hoop-and-Scallom" work.

Lapping or Wrapping.—The transverse skein binding used to cover a handle-bow, frame, or other part of a wicker article.

Leader.—A whole rod or skein carried across a handle or other lapped part and used to form a pattern.

14

PLATE 1 : CORRECT POSITIONS FOR WORKING

PLATE 2: *Above:* ROUND WHITE BREAD OR FRUIT BASKET
Below: CLOSE-RANDED BUFF PICNIC BASKET

Pair.—Formed by working two rods alternately, the left-hand rod being taken over the right, behind the stake, and to the front again.

Picking.—Cutting off surplus ends. Is usually performed in one operation after a complete part such as a bottom, body, or lid has been made.

Piecing-In.—Joining a new rod to one that has been worked to its end.

Randing.—Working a single rod or skein before and behind alternate stakes or bottom or lid sticks.

Round.—A row. A complete circuit of the piece of work, e.g. one round of pairing, four rounds of upsetting.

Scallom.—A rod which has been fixed at right angles to a stouter one by looping its thinned end round it.

Siding.—Applied to any form of weaving used to build up the sides of a basket.

Slath.—A round or oval bottom at the stage when the sticks have been opened out.

Slew.—Similar to randing except that two or more rods are worked together, one above the other.

Slype.—The taper or point formed by two cuts at the end of a rod.

Stakes.—The rods which form the uprights in the sides of a basket.

Sticks.—Pieces of stout rod used to form the framework of a bottom or lid.

Stroke.—Any complete movement in basket-work, e.g. the working of a randing-rod behind a stake and to the front again. Analogous to a stitch in needlework.

Top.—The thin end of a willow rod.

Upsett.—The rounds of waling, put on immediately after the stakes have been turned up, to "set up" the basket.

Wale.—Three or more rods worked in a manner similar to pairing, the left-hand rod being taken each time, carried over the others, behind the stake, and to the front again.

METHODS OF WEAVING

THE principal tools of the basket-maker are his hands, the most important member being the left thumb. The main part of the work is done from left to right, the right hand manipulating the rod which is being worked, and the left hand following up, with the thumb in front and the forefinger at the back. In the case of rectangular bottoms and lids the weaving is done backwards and forwards, so that in alternate rows the positions of the hands are reversed. The main difference between cane and willow is the tendency of the latter to "kink," i.e. to form an angle instead of a curve when bent. This is a valuable property in the willow, making for tightness and resiliency in the finished basket, always providing that the kinks occur in the right places, usually upon the stouter rods round which the others are being worked. It is incorrect to work a stroke loosely, and then, by pushing and pulling, to attempt to tighten it afterwards, for it will have been kinked in the wrong place, and when a kink is once formed the rod loses for good its resiliency in the part that has been kinked.

It is now proposed to deal with all the forms of weaving used in fine willow basket-work, thus saving repetition in subsequent pages.

Randing (Diagram 1).—The blackberry basket on Plate 5 is randed, as are some of the other examples. The picnic basket is close randed, the other randed baskets being light randed. In light randing the rods just touch each other; in close randing they are closed tightly together. In the case of bottoms and lids of rectangular work, a new rod is added by its butt where the top of the old rod finishes, both butt and top resting against one and the same stick on inside or back of work. But in siding a different method is used. The rods are not worked continuously round and round the basket, as with cane, but each new butt is laid in against the stake to the right of that against which the preceding butt was laid (or the rod may be slyped and pushed

16

down alongside stake, which is called Prick Randing). About half an inch of the butt is left on inside of work, to be cut off later. The randing rod is held in the right hand like a pencil at a point about two inches from stake. Now, holding the rod in position against the stake with the left thumb, lift the rod and pass it between the two stakes, pushing it round the back of the right-hand stake with the right thumb and catching it and bringing it to the front again on the right of this stake. All randing, and slewing also, consists in a repetition of these movements, the basket being turned from right to left as the randing proceeds. Randing rods should not reach quite round the basket or the tops will overlap the butts. When a rod has been worked to within a couple of inches or so of its top, this top is left outside basket. These surplus tops, and the butts on inside of basket are cut off when the basket is Picked.

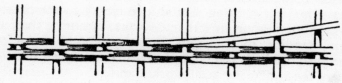

Diagram 1.—RANDING

In siding a basket the stakes should remain straight, the siding being bent to pass in and out of them. The stakes should also be level with each other, that is to say, they must not become corrugated, and must also be kept at the proper distances apart. The stakes should be at least double the thicknes of the randing rods.

When depth of basket is reached at one point, it is "levelled off" by adding extra rods or parts of rods to make the depth even all round.

Close-randing is worked in the same way as light-randing, except that the iron is in frequent use to close the work down quite tightly. Randing rods are proportionately thinner and stakes closer together than in light randing.

Rib-Randing.—This is produced by carrying the randing rod in front of two stakes instead of one, as in ordinary randing. Each rod can be worked in this way throughout its whole length, passing alternately in front of two stakes

17

and behind one, or a part only of each rod can be so worked, the remainder being worked out as ordinary randing. In the soiled-linen basket described on page 42 a spiral rib is formed by taking the butt of each successive randing rod in front of two stakes, behind one, and in front of two again and then working it out in the ordinary way.

French Randing.—The siding of the bread or fruit basket on Plate 2 was done in this way. The method of starting the randing rod is entirely different from that of ordinary randing, all the butts being at the bottom of the siding. This is accomplished by laying the first butt behind a stake and carrying it in front of the next, behind the next, and to the front as in ordinary randing. The second butt is now laid in to the *left* of the first, worked one stroke, and then dropped like the first, and all the other butts are started in the same way, each being worked one stroke and then dropped, the first one being lifted to allow the last one to be put in. Continue now by working a rod one stroke, dropping it, working the one on its left one stroke, dropping that, and so on, randing to the right, but working to the left in picking up each successive rod. This is continued until the tops of the rods have been worked out.

Pairing (Diagram 2).—This is used mainly in round and oval bottoms, and is not suitable for siding. A pair should not finish at the butt ends of the two rods, or a gap is left in

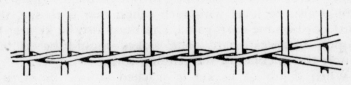

Diagram 2.—PAIRING

the work. This introduces Piecing-in of new rods as follows: The left-hand one of the old butts is pulled to the left and a new butt pushed through the work alongside it. Now take a stroke with this new rod and piece-in the other rod, thus forming a new pair with which the work is continued.

Slewing (Diagram 3).—A two-rod slew was used in the siding of the oval garden basket, and a three-rod slew in the oval buff shopping basket, both on Plate 5. Slewing is worked continuously round and round the basket, and an odd number of stakes is necessary. Two-rod slewing is begun with a single rod as in randing, and when this rod has been worked for half its length a second rod is laid in above it, and the two worked together. When the lower rod runs out, its top is left on outside of basket and a third butt is laid in above the other rod, between the same two stakes, to

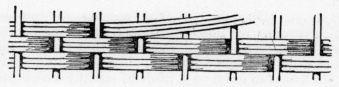

Diagram 3.—SLEWING (THREE-ROD)

make the slewing rods up to two again. In the same way a fourth rod is laid in when the second runs out, and so on. Three-rod slewing is begun in the same way, but a second butt is added when about one-third of the first rod has been worked, and a third rod when about two-thirds of the first has been worked. This gives the three rods, and the number is maintained by adding a butt above the others when a top finishes below.

French Slewing.—Shown in round buff shopping basket on Plate 4. Either two or three rods may be used, these being worked as one in the same way as French randing.

In any form of slewing, rods thinner in proportion to the stakes than those used for randing are desirable, as the pressure of two or more rods is naturally greater than that of one rod.

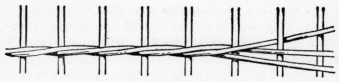

Diagram 4.—THREE-ROD WALE

Waling (Diagrams 4 and 5).—Waling is worked on the same principle as pairing, piecing-in tops to tops, and butts to butts, and finishing with tops. In addition to the three-

19

rod and four-rod waling illustrated, five-rod and six-rod waling is sometimes used. Wale rods may be nearly as stout as the stakes. The wale can be produced on inside of basket by taking each rod in front of one stake and behind the next two (or three if a four-rod wale), or with four rods the wale can be produced both inside and outside the basket by taking each rod in front of two stakes and behind the next two.

Upsetting (Diagram 5).—The number of rounds of waling forming the upsetting should, in fine basket-work, never be less than two, and seldom less than three. It will be found easier to begin with tops, although a stronger edge for the basket to stand on is made by starting with butts. In either case the ends are not laid in, but slyped and pushed

Diagram 5.—Four-Rod Waling used as First Round of Upsetting

into the bottom by the sides of three or four adjoining stakes. The first round of upsetting on larger baskets is usually a four-rod one, one rod being dropped on the completion of the first round, and the remainder of upsett worked with three rods. No piecing-in should be done in the first round, and if the rods are not long enough to go right round the basket, with a little to spare, begin with two sets of rods on opposite sides of the basket. The tendency in upsetting is to allow the work to splay out too much and it is in the second round that this tendency is most apparent. This second round should, therefore, be worked inwards more than would appear to be necessary in any given basket.

Fitching (Diagrams 6, 7, 8, and 9).—This is the term for open work in basket-work, and is accomplished by working two rods as a Fitch to secure the stakes above the open part. The two main kinds are straight fitching (Diagram 7) and cross fitching. A pleasing combination of the two is shown in Diagram 6. The fitch is usually begun by placing the tops

20

of two rods of equal size and length together and looping
them round a stake (Diagram 8). In working the fitch, the
rod away from worker is grasped with the right hand and
brought over the other rod towards him, this other rod
being held between the forefinger and thumb of the left
hand, palm uppermost, the rods changing from hand to

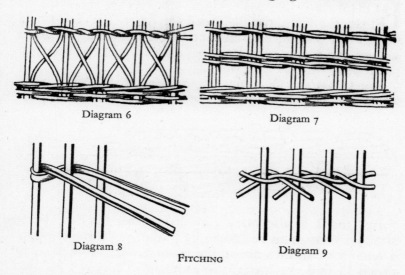

Diagram 6

Diagram 7

Diagram 8

FITCHING

Diagram 9

hand after each stroke. The size of the fitch rods is generally
a little smaller than that of the stakes, and if necessary a
double turn is taken between each two stakes, as shown in
Diagram 6. When the butts of the first two fitch rods are
reached two more butts are pieced-in, as shown in Diagram
9. When a round of fitching is completed, the remainder of
the two rods may be worked out as a pair, or a wale can be
worked by adding a third rod.

BORDERS AND HANDLES

BORDERS.—The main kinds of border are the Track or Trac, the Plain, the Plait, and the Rope. The Scallop or Openwork border, used in cane work, is difficult to do in willow, is perhaps more "pretty" than artistic, and does not wear well.

Track Borders (Diagrams 10, 11, and 12).—Many variations are possible in this type of border, one of its simplest

Diagram 10.—SIMPLE TRACK BORDER

forms, used in the blackberry basket on Plate 5, being shown by Diagram 10. Begin by kinking two stakes about a quarter of an inch above the waling, then bring the first down behind the second, in front of the next two, and leave it behind the fifth. Repeat with each stake in succession, threading the last ones into position to correspond with the

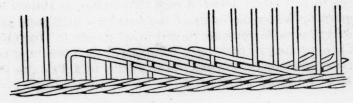

Diagram 11.—ANOTHER TRACK BORDER

remainder. Diagram 11 shows a track border somewhat more complex than the foregoing, used in the round buff shopping basket on Plate 4. Each stake is taken in front of the next two, behind one, and in front of two again, the end being left inside as before. It is a good plan to cut off each end as it is finished with, just long enough to rest against

22

the stake. In beginning this border, five or six stakes are kinked down at the correct height by inserting the point of the hand-knife half-way into the stake, and giving it a half turn as stake is brought down. Each of the other stakes is brought down with the fingers, which grip the stake and give it a half turn or twist as it is brought down, to prevent it cracking.

Diagram 12.—TRACK BORDER WITH DOUBLE STAKES

Diagram 12 shows the previous border worked with an additional stake pushed into the basket by the side of each existing stake before the border is begun.

Plain Borders (Diagrams 13 and 14).—These comprise the Two-Rod, Three-Rod, Four-Rod, Five-Rod, and (occasionally) Six-Rod. In each case the stake can be brought down either behind the next one or the next two, the resulting borders being described here as "Behind-One" and "Behind-Two" respectively.

Two-Rod Plain Border.—This is used on ends of picnic-basket lid, Plate 2, but is not often used to "border off" the

Diagram 13.—THREE-ROD-BEHIND-ONE PLAIN BORDER

sides of a basket, unless it is a very small one. In the case of a basket, say, a small early attempt, begin by bringing down any two stakes each behind either the next one or the next two stakes. Calling these stakes Nos. 1 and 2, and the next ones on their right Nos. 3, 4, and 5, and using the Behind-One method, proceed as follows: Carry No. 1 in front of No. 3, behind No. 4, and to the front. Then bring down No. 3 behind No. 4 and to the front, side by side and close to No. 1. Now take No. 2 in front of No. 4, behind No. 3, and to the front, and bring down No. 4 alongside it. This gives two pairs, and the border is continued by taking the right-hand rod of the left-hand pair each time, and working it as described for the first two rods. The left-hand rod of each pair is left to be cut off later. When the work comes round to the starting point, and only one stake is left standing, proceed as follows: Thread the right-hand rod of the left-hand pair through under the kink of No. 1 stake, and bring down the upstanding stake, and thread it through to the front close alongside the other rod. This gives two pairs once again. Take the right-hand rod of the left-hand pair in front of the stake against which it rests and kink it at right angles at a point just to the left of the next stake, slype the rod about an inch from the kink, and insert the slype into the basket to the left of, and alongside, the stake, driving it down with a

Diagram 14.—Four-Rod-Behind-Two Plain Border

light tap or two with the iron. The right-hand rod of the remaining pair is dealt with in the same way, thus completing the border by the method known as "cramming off."

Three-Rod Border (Diagram 13).—This is begun by bringing down three stakes instead of two, and continued in the same way as the two-rod border, except that the front stroke is before two stakes instead of one, and there is an additional cram at the finish. The right-hand rod of the pair on the left is taken each time, its fellow being left as before.

Four-Rod (Diagram 14) *and Five-Rod Borders.*—Four-rod borders are used in the round white bread basket and the picnic basket on Plate 2, and five-rod borders in the soiled-linen basket and the cycle basket, Plate 4. In these borders, and to a lesser degree in the three-rod, the first strokes should not be worked tightly, but looped out somewhat to leave room for the finishing crams.

24

Plait Border (Diagrams 15 and 16).—The diagrams show how one of the simpler forms of plait border is accomplished, this border being used for the oblong buff work basket on Plate 3. Plait borders can be varied by having three rods together instead of two, by increasing the number of pairs or threes used, and by varying the number of stakes before and behind which the pair or three passes. For the border illustrated, two short butts are used as

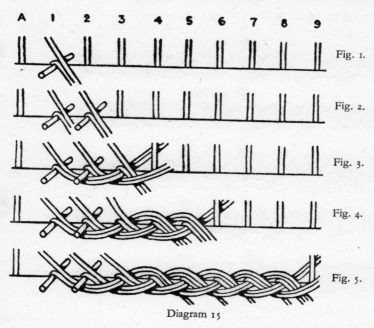

Diagram 15

temporary pegs, one of which is placed between two stakes with its inner end pointing to the right. Bring the stake down over it to the front, and by the side of this stake lay a rod of the same size with a portion of the butt end projecting on the inside of the work. Now insert the next peg in the second space, bring down No. 2 stake over it and add a second rod as before. Of the two pairs thus formed take the left-hand one over the other, in front of No. 3 stake, and leave it on the inside. Bring down No. 3 stake and add a rod, this giving the three pairs necessary for the border, two being now at the front and one at the back. Now repeat the following strokes: Take the left-hand pair of the two in front over the right-hand pair, in front of the first upright stake, and to the inside, leaving it there. Bring down the stake over this pair to the front, and then take the left-hand pair of the two at the back and bring it to the front on the right of the stake just laid down, and side by side with it. The *right-hand* rod of the three is now finished with, the other two being taken when their turn comes. To finish the

D   C   B   A   1   2   3   4   5   6

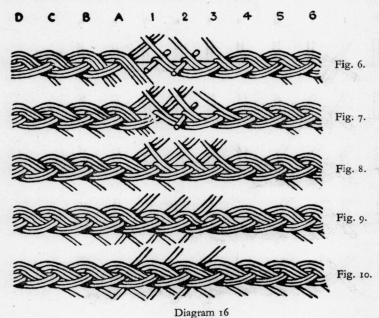

Fig. 6.

Fig. 7.

Fig. 8.

Fig. 9.

Fig. 10.

Diagram 16

border remove the pegs, and thread the two pairs that are in front through to the back in their proper places, as shown by Fig. 8. The butts of the extra rods are now threaded through to the front as shown in Fig. 9, and the border completed by threading the right-hand rod of each pair through to the front, as shown by Fig. 10.

Rope Border.—This is simple in construction, and the only variation is obtained by inserting more extra rods at the beginning to form thicker twists. The simplest and smallest rope border was used on the oval buff shopping basket, Plate 5, and this is begun by inserting an extra rod by the side of each of two adjoining stakes. The left-hand pair of rods is then brought down to the front, twisted upon themselves in an anti-clockwise direction, and taken through to the inside between the upstanding pair and the first single stake, where they are left for the time being. Now treat the other pair in the same way, taking it through between the first and second single stakes and leaving it there. Then bring the left-hand pair to the front on the right of the first upright stake, which is brought down and twisted with them, the three-rod twist being taken through to the back as before. After this the other pair is treated in the same way, so that there are two threes at the back. The shortest rod of each three is henceforth left on the inside, the remaining two being brought forward and twisted with the stake to form another three, the whole of the border being simply a repetition of the foregoing strokes. On reaching the starting point, a neat finish is made by threading the last pair through under the first doubled stake, and then threading one rod of each of the two threes into position in the two-rod twists with which the border was begun.

A method of combining the plain and track borders is illustrated by the tray on Plate 5. A "four-rod-behind-one" border was worked in the ordinary way, except that, instead of being crammed off, the last strokes were drawn through. The ends were then worked to form a simple track, each rod being brought out at right angles to the border, taken over the next two, under the next, over the next, and its end left underneath.

Handles.—These are of two main kinds: Cross Handles and Small Handles. Both can be either Roped or Lapped. Lapped handles are dealt with in the section on Skein Work. Roped Cross handles may be either Whole-Rod or Twisted-Rod.

Twisted-Rod Cross Handles.—The blackberry basket, Plate 5, has a handle of this kind, which requires a bow of stout rod fitted across the basket from side to side or end to end by inserting its slyped ends down into the siding, alongside two stakes or into Bow Marks. These are formed by working the siding in front of and behind two stakes, as shown in oval buff shopping basket, Plate 5. The bow marks are kept open temporarily by means of short pieces of rod placed inside them to keep the stakes apart. The left-hand stake of each two is not bordered down like the remainder, but left standing to be cut off later. Having inserted the bow, select four sound rods, long enough to go twice across the bow with a little to spare, and push their slyped butts down alongside the bow, to its left and close to it, two on either side of basket. The front rod of one of the pairs is now twisted throughout its length, beginning at top of rod and twisting with the forefinger and thumb of the right hand in a clockwise direction, the left hand holding the rod a little lower down. If the rod is a small one the twisting can be so continued right down to the butt, but in the case of a larger rod it is necessary, in order to obtain a better purchase, to form the twisted top into a sort of crank and turn it as one would a handle. In either case, after twisting an inch or two the hands are moved lower down, the twisted part being allowed to untwist again temporarily. Now coil the first twisted rod four or five times round the bow, retwisting it as necessary, and take it through under the border from the outside and to the left of the bow on opposite side of basket. This rod is left for the time being and one from this side is twisted and taken over to the other side, keeping each stroke close to the corresponding one of the first rod. The other two rods are twisted and worked in turn, and then each of them is taken across the bow again, threaded through the opening just above the border, and cut off; or, to give a neater finish, they can be taken through under border and threaded in and out of the stakes for a short way.

Whole-Rod Cross Handle.—This was used on the round buff shopping basket on Plate 4, and is worked as follows: Select six or eight rods (according to the size of the handle and of the rods) long enough to go once across the bow, with six or eight inches to spare, and insert three (or four) close against the bow, beginning on its left with the first rod and adding the others towards inside of basket, close to the bow and to each other. Do the same with the other three (or four) rods at the other side, and then, taking one set at a time (or if this is found too difficult, one rod at a time) coil them four or five times round the bow, keeping each set of rods together. To finish the handle the rods of each set are cut off level near their tops, and taken in turn through under the border to the left of the bow, over the top of the border on the same side, and then through under the border on the right, where they are twisted together and threaded under the border for one or two strokes.

Twisted Single-Rod Small Handle.—Small handles can be placed either on the border or below it. Those below the borders are put on before border is laid down, and are, with slight modifications, worked in the same way as those above border. For a single-rod handle on the border a rod, long enough to go three times across handle, is slyped and pushed into the border at the point which will be the right-hand side of handle. The rod is then twisted and taken through under border from the outside at the place where left-hand side of handle is to be (the loop thus formed being large enough to accommodate the fingers comfortably), taken three or four times round the loop, and then through under the border from the outside, then worked back again, and taken through the space in handle just above border and cut off or threaded along under border. In this handle the effect should be that of a three-strand rope.

Twisted Double-Rod Small Handle.—For this type of handle, used on the round white bread basket, Plate 2, two rods are used, these being inserted into the border at the required distance apart. The right-hand rod is taken through under the border as before, but without being twisted, as it is the function of this first rod to form a bow. The left-hand rod is now twisted and taken three times round the bow, then through under the border and back again, and again taken through under the border to the left of the bow. The bow rod is now twisted, worked across to the right, taken under the border on the right of the other rod, worked across to the left again, and drawn through just above the border. The other rod, which was temporarily dropped, is now worked over to the right, and drawn through just above the border also.

SKEIN WORK

SKEINS, which are thin strips of split willow, are easy to work, and their use, in combination with whole rods, is to be recommended to those whose hands are not equal to the task of working whole rods throughout. Skeins, either white or buff (brown is not used for this purpose), may be made by the worker. The processes are as follows:

Cleaving.—Dry rods are used for skein-making, which is begun at the top of the rod, six inches or so of which is cut off first. Cuts are then made with the hand-knife to accommodate the cleave, which is pressed along the rod with the right hand, spaces being left between the fingers to allow the clefts to pass. The rod is held a little lower down by the left hand, which is moved downwards as the cleaving proceeds. The operation is one of rending or splitting, not cutting, and the cleave must be guided aright to ensure that the three clefts are equal in size.

Shaving.—The ordinary method is to sit with the shave grasped in the left hand, resting against the left knee, but an easier way is to fix the shave to table top. The cleft is drawn through pith side uppermost with the right hand, while the left thumb (protected by a thumb-stall) holds the cleft down on the far side of the cutting edge. First grasp the cleft at about its centre and draw the butt end through the shave, and then reverse the cleft and draw through the other part, holding the butt end which has already been shaved. For ordinary purposes each cleft will be shaved twice, the shave being screwed up tighter for the second shaving; but if very thin skeins are required, or the clefts are extra large, three or four times may be necessary. To save time, all the clefts should be drawn through before the shave is altered.

Uprighting.—For most skein work the skeins are used after being shaved, but for extra fine work they are made uniform in width, and as narrow as required, by being drawn through the Upright. The two cutting edges of this tool must be carefully set at exactly the same angle, and the skein, which is drawn through with the right hand and held down with the left thumb as in shaving, must be carefully guided. In uprighting it is the skin side of the skein that is uppermost. The top of the skein is placed between the two knives, and the uprighting is completed in one operation by pulling the skein through to its butt. References to the butt and top of a skein in the following pages do not, of course, apply to uprighted skeins, both ends of which are alike.

Skein Slath for Round Bottom or Lid.—We now begin actual working instructions, and the learner will get best results by studying them with the work in hand; indeed, a great part of them will simply bewilder him unless he does so. Another aid to the understanding of these written directions (which are necessarily very much less effective than oral tuition) is to examine as many specimens of basket-work as possible. Having watered some material suitable for a small round practice basket, and made some skeins, cut six bottom-sticks from the butt ends of six of the stouter rods, two inches longer than the diameter of the bottom it is proposed to make. Pierce three of these in their centres with the hand-knife or bodkin, and thread the other three through them to form a cross as shown in Diagram 17. Now insert the top of a skein in the split to the left of one of the three, pass it in front of this three, behind the next three, in front of the next, and behind the next. The skein is now taken diagonally across from corner to corner and again at the back, returning to the point at which the first diagonal started. It is now taken to the left over the first three, behind the next three, and in front of the next three.

Another diagonal is then formed at right angles to the first by carrying the skein over to the opposite corner, then across again at the back, forming another diagonal, again at right angles to the previous one. The "tying-in" part of the slath is completed by taking the skein behind the three to its left, which gives a cross within a square at both front and back (Diagram 18). All round and oval bottoms are made slightly convex or saucer-shaped, therefore the sticks in the present bottom will be curved somewhat towards worker as the work proceeds, that side of the bottom which is now towards worker being underneath in the finished basket. The side away from worker is the "right" side of bottom, and on this side the ribbing which is now to be worked will appear. At this point it may be noted that what can be called Flat-Skein Work is being used, each stroke lying as nearly as possible flatly upon the one underneath. In what may be termed Edge-Skein Work, referred to below, the skeins are worked edge to edge. Diagram 18 is, for the sake of clearness, made to appear as edge-skein work, but in the actual bottom only the edges of the skeins would be seen.

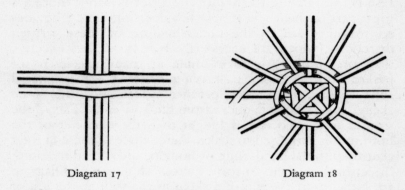

Diagram 17   Diagram 18

The next stage of the work is the "opening out" of the sticks, which, in the present bottom, is begun by taking the skein through to the back on the right of the left-hand stick of the first three, this stick being pulled to the left away from the other two. The skein now goes behind the next two sticks and to the front again, and the other groups of threes are opened out in the same way into ones and twos. Before doing the second round it is necessary to pass the skein in front of two sticks, once only, so that in the next round each stroke will pass behind a different two sticks, thus opening out all the sticks singly and forming ribbing on the "right" side of the bottom. As each round is completed the skein is taken in front of two sticks once only, the remainder of the work being a repetition of the "in front of one and behind two" stroke. Diagram 18 shows the *reversed* slath when all the sticks have been opened out, after which the skein ribbing can be continued for part or the whole of the bottom, or two rods can be inserted by their tops to the left of two adjoining sticks, and the bottom completed with pairing. In piecing-in additional skeins in a round or oval bottom, the method shown by Diagram 19 is used. Instead of completing the bottom with flat-skein work or rod pairing, it can be done with skeins worked edge to edge as in siding, these being worked either as ordinary randing or to form ribbing as at the beginning. Skein slaths can be used instead of rod ones in the other round and oval baskets, the method of setting out the bottom sticks of an oval bottom being given in the instructions for the oval garden basket (page 45).

Edge-Skein Work.—This is shown in the siding of the oblong baby's or work basket, Plate 3, and by Diagram 19.

The method of piecing-in in siding is, however, different from that shown in this diagram of part of a bottom. In siding, the end of the old skein and that of the new are worked together for two strokes, the new end lying flat against

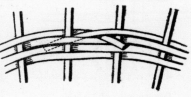

Diagram 19

the other, and in front of it, so that the two occupy no more space vertically than one skein. The end of the new skein will be left at the front of the work, and the old one at the back, both being cut off close when the basket is picked.

Skein Lapping or Wrapping.—Lapping is one of the principal ways in which skeins are used, their flatness and thinness making them very suitable for this purpose, the thinner the skein the more easy being the work. Among other things, lapping is used for covering legs and other parts of wicker furniture and for basket handles as described below. Plain lapping on a frame such as is used, for example, for a cake stand is begun as shown in Diagram 20, a quarter-inch or half-inch fine nail securing the skein just under the bend. Lapping is done from left to right, the skein passing over top of frame away from worker, the right hand being used to manipulate the skein while the left thumb and forefinger hold each lap as it is completed. Diagram 21 shows the end being bound in with the lapping, and Diagrams 22 and 23 show the method of piecing-in a new skein, which is done as follows: When about eight inches of the old skein remains, place the new end along the frame, cut side outwards, and proceed to lap this in until only about two inches of the old skein remains. Holding this in the right hand, and the new skein in the left, turn the skeins so that the new one comes over the old, and in position to continue the lapping, and the old end lies along the frame, cut side outwards, to be bound in when lapping is continued. To finish off, the end is passed under the last

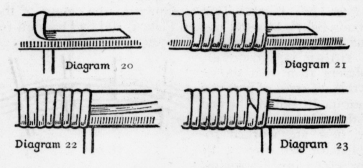

Diagram 20   Diagram 21

Diagram 22   Diagram 23

lap and drawn tight, a nail is inserted where the two parts cross, and the end cut off close. Lapping with skeins is done in precisely the same way as with pulp or centre cane, so that fuller information can be found in the book on cane work published by the Dryad Press.

Skein Handles.—All skein handles have a bow or bows, the lapping being done in the way described above except for the beginning and ending. To begin a lapped handle such as that on oval buff shopping basket, Plate 5, push down the sharpened butt of a skein on the right of the bow, take its top through under the border on the left, up over the border to the front on the same side, then under the border to the inside on the right of the bow, and up over the border on this side ready to begin the lapping. This forms a cross on the outside of basket. The handle is finished on the other side with a cross to correspond, and the end of skein worked along under border to secure it.

Small handles (Diagrams 24 and 25) are done in a similar way.

Leaders.—These are shown on all the lapped handles illustrated. They are used, firstly, to introduce pattern to relieve the plain lapping and, secondly, to hold the handle securely to the basket as an alternative to, or in addition to, pegging. For the latter purpose the butt end of a leader-rod (skeins are not strong enough for this purpose, though ideal for forming pattern) is cut to a long tongue as in

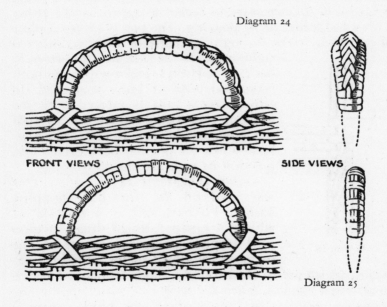

Diagram 24

FRONT VIEWS   SIDE VIEWS

Diagram 25

scalloming. This tongue is then pushed up between the waling and the bow, cut side outwards, and the remainder of rod brought up in front, thus formimg a secure loop round the waling and the border. A cross and plain lapping is then worked for a distance of at least two inches, after which the leader (or leaders) is used to form a pattern by passing the lapping skein over and under it (or them) in a variety of ways. When within about two inches of the other side, the leader-rod is cut to a long tongue as before, and this is pushed up between wale and bow to correspond with the beginning, the handle being then finished with plain lapping and a cross. If one or more skeins instead of rods are used as leaders, these are pushed in under the plain lapping and their ends bound in with the plain lapping with which the handle is finished. Diagram 25 shows the use of two leaders. More than two leaders can be used in wider pieces of lapping, and the lapping can pass over all the leaders at once or over some and under others in the same lap. Diamonds, chequers, and other interesting patterns can be worked, either singly or in combination, and if dyed skeins are used, variety of colour can be introduced as well. It is absolutely necessary to secure a lapped handle either with a rod-leader or by pegging. The peg is simply a piece of butt end, driven through the centre of the bow, either at right angles to the side, i.e. from front to back, or sideways, passing through both stake and bow or bows if desired. In either case a hole is pierced with the bodkin, care being taken not to split the bow, or the peg is practically useless. When the peg has been driven into position its ends are cut off close.

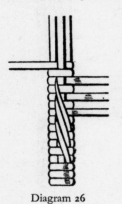

Diagram 26

Listing (Diagrams 24 and 26).—This was used on the oval buff shopping basket, Plate 5, and is a method of adding a raised form of ornamentation to a lapped handle by the use of one or more additional skeins, called listing-skeins, which are worked round a single whole-rod leader. In all listed handles, when the section of plain lapping just above the border has been worked, the lapping-skein is taken once over and once under the leader alternately, a listing-skein coming up and round under the leader each time the lapping-skein goes under it. Diagram 26 shows a simple listed handle employing three listing-skeins, seen on the right. After the ends of the listing-skeins have been bound in as shown, the listing proceeds until other side of handle is reached, when the listing-skeins are bound in one by one to correspond with the beginning, and the handle is finished with plain lapping and a cross as usual. Diagram 24 shows listing-skeins worked from either side to form a herring-bone pattern. The listing on any handle can be added after the handle has been lapped over and under the leader alternately, spaces being made under the leader with the bodkin to enable the listing-skeins to be threaded through.

ROUND WORK

*B*ROWN *and White Blackberry Basket* (Plate 5, Diagrams 27 and 28).—Before beginning the actual
making of a piece of work, the "cutting out" (a workshop
term which includes the sorting of the material into sizes
suitable for the various parts of the article) should be carefully attended to. If two or more articles of the same kind
are to be made, time will be saved and more uniform
results secured if the "stuff" (another workshop term
applied to any kind of basket material) for the total
number is cut out at one operation. Having soaked
some two-feet to three-feet white and some brown
of a smaller size (or white only can be used) and
allowed this to lie under the damp sacking till mellow, place the white on the left of the table and, with
remainder of the table top clear and the hand-knife
in the right hand, proceed to pick up the rods one
by one with the left hand, and place them in separate
piles according to the purpose they are to serve in
the basket, those that require it being cut at the same
time. This avoids the time-wasting process of picking over the bundle later to find a rod for a particular
purpose. The brown stuff can be left on the floor for
Diagram the present. From the butt ends of five of the stoutest
27   rods, bottom-sticks are cut six inches long, the
remaining portions of the rods being slyped for stakes. The
bottom-sticks can be cut off with the shears, but the slyping
of the stakes is done with the hand-knife, the rod being held
with the left hand, and the cutting done towards the worker.
Diagram 27 shows the slype, which is made by two cuts,
one on the face of the rod and one other on the left or the
right. Fifteen other stakes are slyped as and when suitable
rods are taken from the bundle. Similarly, rods suitable for
bottoming, siding, waling, and the handle are laid in
separate piles to be tied up when the whole of the bundle
has been distributed. Not quite such an elaborate process is

absolutely necessary in the present instance, but experience has shown the desirability of making a general practice of cutting out, adapting this to the work in hand.

The actual making of the present example is begun by piercing two of the bottom-sticks in their centres and threading the other three through them, after which the slath can be formed either with skeins, as described earlier, or with rods as follows: Take two thin rods of the same size and length and insert both tops (from which a little can be cut) into the split on the left of a group of three, and work round three times, using the method of pairing. With the fourth round the sticks are opened out, the groups of two into singles, and the threes into a two and a one. Begin the separation of each group by taking the rod right down behind it as though the previous working were to be continued, and hold it there with the left forefinger. Remove the right hand from the rod altogether and bring it to the front. Separate the sticks with this hand and, placing it between them, bring the rod through to the front; then, and not till then, release the pressure of the left forefinger.

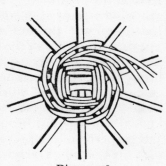

Diagram 28

The worker need not be discouraged if he fails to open out tightly and neatly at the first few attempts, for although round work is on the whole the simplest, this particular part of it is one of the most difficult operations in basket-work. With the next and fifth round, the twos are opened out so that all the sticks are separated, and the remainder of the bottom consists of pairing round and round, as shown by Diagram 28. When the butts of the first pair are reached, two more butts are pieced-in to them in adjoining spaces by pushing each new butt through to the left of the old one, as shown by Diagram 19 which illustrates the method applied to randing. In the present basket the brown stuff is used for the remainder of the bottom, which is four inches in diameter, butts being pieced-in to butts, and tops to tops. When the correct diameter is reached the pair-rods are slyped and pushed through to the front just under the previous round of pairing, the bottom sticks are cut off with the shears and the bottom is picked. In picking, the angle made with the work is about 45 degrees, and pressure just sufficient to sever the end is exerted. This is not easy at first, and the shears may be used where practicable, and will always be used in cases such as the cutting off of the butts of fitch rods, where great risk would be run of cutting the stakes or other parts of the work with the picking-knife. Ends should be cut as closely as possible, but not so close that they have nothing to rest upon.

The next process is Staking-Up, which is performed on the table-top with concave or hollow side of bottom uppermost at the beginning, a stake being pushed into the bottom on either side of each stick-end. The bottom is now turned the other way up and the stakes kinked-up sharply by inserting the point of the hand-knife just beyond the edge of the bottom, and giving the knife a half turn as the stake is brought up, thus opening it out so that it will bend without cracking (hence the workshop term "pricking-up"). Each stake is allowed to fall back again, and when all have been kinked up they are brought into a vertical position again and gathered into a previously prepared hoop a little larger than the bottom. The hoop is prevented from slipping off by passing one or two stakes through between its coils.

All the stakes are now tapped in close with the flat of the iron, and the upsett is begun by inserting the slyped tops of three white rods, about two-thirds the thickness of the stakes, and equal in size and length with each other. These three are now worked to their butts, the first round being worked well in between the stakes and bottom-sticks. When the first round has been completed the bottom is pegged to the work-board. Waling is continued with the three rods until their butts are reached, when three more butts are pieced-in and worked out to their tops, which completes the upsett for this basket, approximately three rounds.

The hoop ought now to be removed, but if the stakes have been allowed to splay out too much it may be kept on till an inch or two of randing has been worked. When the hoop has been removed the ultimate diameter of the basket is tested by measuring across between opposite stakes at what is to be the depth of the basket, in this case five inches, with an inside top diameter of six inches. It may be mentioned here that inside measurements are generally used for basket-ware, but for convenience the depth is usually taken on the outside, when the basket is being made, the difference between inside and outside measurements being allowed for. The brown stuff is now laid on the right-hand side and used to rand the basket to a depth of three inches, the work being levelled-off all round at this depth. A piece of rod cut to the required length and used as a gauge is very useful in levelling-off. Next about three-quarters of an inch of white randing is worked to give variety, this being followed by a little more brown to bring the depth to four and a half inches, at which depth it is levelled-off and about two rounds of top waling are put on, beginning with three tops, and ending with the three tops of a second set of three rods, pieced-in butts to butts to the first three. The stakes are now damped and brought down to form a simple track border. The basket is now picked both inside and out, and completed by the putting on of a white twisted-rod cross handle.

Round White Bread or Fruit Basket, Plate 2.—For making this basket, rods from a bundle of three-foot stuff will be suitable. The bottom is eight inches in diameter and has eight bottom-sticks, four across four. Tying-in is begun with two tops as before, and when these have been paired round three times, each group of four sticks is opened into two twos. Two rounds of pairing are worked with the sticks in twos, and with the sixth round they are opened out singly and pairing continued until bottom is eight inches in diameter, butts being pieced-in to butts and tops to tops as before. There are thirty-two stakes and three rounds of upsetting, the latter being begun with four butts, slyped and inserted into bottom side by side with four adjoining stakes. When the first round is completed one rod is dropped, and the upsett continued with three rods. Three more tops are pieced-in to the first three, and three more butts when the butts of the second three are reached, this third set completing the upsett of about three rounds. During the upsetting of this basket the stakes must be brought well out, as there is a pronounced flow in the sides, the inside diameter at three and a half inches deep being eleven inches. A French rand is used for the siding of this basket, and two rounds of three-rod top waling are then worked, the wale being produced on inside of basket by taking each stroke behind two stakes and in front of one. Then a four-rod-behind-one border is worked, the basket is picked, and the job completed by putting on two twisted-rod double handles, one being placed over the crams of the border.

Round Buff Shopping Basket, Plate 4.—The material for this ranges from the smallest Dicky Meadows up to rods two feet six inches to three feet for stakes and handle rods. The bottom is five inches in diameter and is made in the same way as the bottom of the bread basket, with eight bottom-sticks. Thirty-two stakes are required, and these are inserted so that when they are turned up the natural curve of the rods will be outwards. There are three rounds of upsetting begun with three tops, and in the doing of this the stakes are brought well out to produce a bowl or barrel shape. After the upsett, a French two-rod slew is worked, then two rounds of top waling and the track border shown by Diagram 11. This basket has a whole-rod handle The inside top measurement is nine inches, but this can be less according to the style of basket desired. It should not be more in a shopping basket of this type.

Round Buff Soiled-Linen Basket.—This is a larger and more advanced example, although as soiled-linen baskets go it is a comparatively small one. The task of keeping the stakes straight and almost upright is not an easy one, so that this basket should not be attempted in the early stages of train-ing. Five-foot stuff is used for the stakes, and rods ranging from about two feet six inches up to four feet six inches for randing, bottoming, upsetting, and waling, and for the lid. The lid has a skein slath, and there are two skein handles on the border. The bottom is ten inches in diameter with ten bottom-sticks, five threaded through five. There are forty stakes and three rounds of upsetting, the latter not being worked in close between stakes and bottom-sticks, but like ordinary waling, a little above the kinks of the stakes. This is to allow for the foot-stakes to be inserted later, and for the

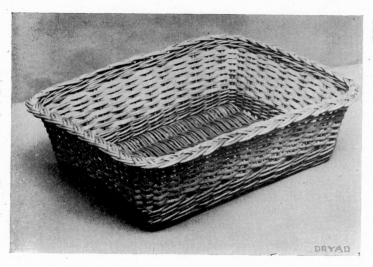

PLATE 3: *Above:* BOAT BASKET AND LIDDED "SOUTHPORT" BASKET
Below: OBLONG BUFF BABY'S OR WORK BASKET

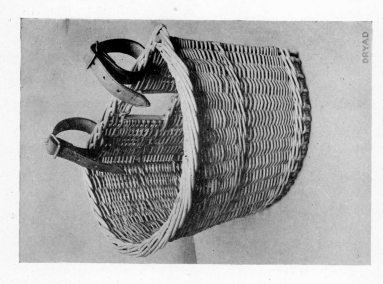

Half-Moon Buff Cycle Basket

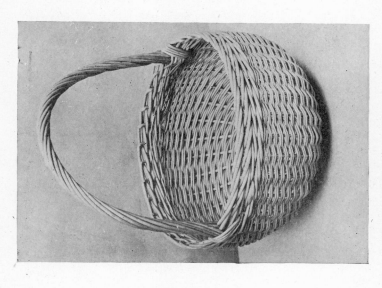

Plate 4: Round Buff Shopping Basket

[43

same reason the upsett is begun with three tops simply laid in. After the upsetting ordinary prick randing (in which each rod is slyped and pushed down by the side of the stake instead of being simply laid in) is worked to a depth of two inches, the basket flowing only slightly, as the inside diameter at top is to be only eleven or twelve inches. After the ordinary prick randing two rounds of three-rod waling are worked, and then rib-randing, the butt of each randing rod being pricked in as before. A spiral rib is formed by carrying the butt of each randing rod in front of two stakes, behind one, in front of two again, and then working the remainder of the rod as ordinary plain randing. When a depth of eleven inches is reached, the work is levelled and two rounds of waling put on, to be followed by another small section of randing to correspond to the lower one, or the whole of the siding may be rib-randing. At a depth of thirteen inches two rounds of waling are worked, and then the stakes are brought out at an angle and five more rounds of waling put on to form the neck, this waling being produced on inside of work. The example has a five-rod-behind-two border, but a plait or a rope border could be substituted.

The basket is now picked and turned upside down to receive the foot. For this, forty stakes, of about the same size as the waling, are slyped and pushed down to the left and right respectively of each pair of the original stakes. Five rounds of ordinary three-rod waling are then worked, the stakes being brought out at an angle to correspond with the neck, and the foot is completed by bringing down the stakes to form a three-rod-behind-two border.

Next, the two lapped skein handles are added, and then the lid is made. This has twelve sticks, threaded six through six, and tied-in and opened-out with skeins as previously described. The skein ribbing is continued to a diameter of four or five inches, a pronounced curve being given to the sticks after they have been opened out. The remainder of the lid is filled out with three-rod waling, both waling and ribbing being produced on the convex or top side of the lid. In the waling, the butts and tops are not pieced in as in ordinary waling, but both old and new ends are simply left on the underside of lid. When a diameter about half an inch less than that of the basket is reached, the ends of the wale rods are drawn through and the sticks cut off. With the top of the lid facing him the worker then inserts a slyped rod to the left of each stick end, and brings them down into a three-rod-behind-one border. The lid is attached to the basket by means of two hinges, separated by about two inches, and placed midway between the two handles. Each of the hinges is worked as follows: A rod is bent in half by placing the blade of the bodkin near its centre and turning the rod upon it, the two ends of the rod being then slyped level with each other. This doubled rod is then pushed through from inside of basket, an end on either side of a stake, just below the top round of waling. The rod is drawn through, its two halves twisted one upon the other, and the twist thus formed is carried up over the border, and down through the lid between the last and last-but-one rounds of waling. The two ends are then taken through on either side of the stake in the same places as at first, and worked along the stakes to secure them. To allow lid to move easily, these hinges must be roomy—what the basket-maker calls "fast and loose." The basket is completed by putting a small three-strand twisted loop on front of lid, this being worked in the same way as a twisted single-rod handle.

OVAL WORK

OVAL Tray with Willow Edging, Plate 5.—Being oval in shape, the tray about to be described is included in this section, but there is no essential difference between this shape and any other as far as the willow work is concerned, except in the case of square-cornered trays, which can have a sharp-cornered border if desired. Willow-edged trays are really nothing else than very shallow baskets with wooden bottoms or bases, so that by including some form of siding, baskets of various depths, shapes, and sizes can be made, all other details being the same as for trays. For the present example buff is used, Dicky Meadows for preference, about two feet long. From a prepared bundle of this, select and slype the required number of stakes, which will be the same as the number of holes in the base. Now, holding the base upright on the lap, insert three stakes in three adjoining holes, butts to the front. The simple track border which forms the foot of the tray is then begun by taking the first stake over the second, and leaving its end under the third, sufficient surplus being left to ensure that when the butts are cut off later, about a quarter of an inch of unslyped rod will be left beyond the stake. A fourth stake is now inserted to the right of the third, the second stake is worked in the same way as the first, a fifth stake is inserted, and so on, right round the base, threading the last butt into position under the first. The work is then placed on the table, and four rounds of three-rod waling put on. To complete the tray, the stakes are brought down to form a four-rod-behind-one border, with ends worked into a "back track," as described under Borders and Handles.

Oval Brown-and-White Garden Basket (Plate 5, Diagram 29).—This example, like the round blackberry basket, represents a relatively small and simple specimen of its kind, but it may be mentioned now, that the reader is not asked to adhere strictly to these and the other examples given, all of which are intended to serve mainly as suggestions, and were designed primarily to include the various kinds of weaving, borders, etc.

For oval bottoms and lids, as well as round ones, the simple and comparatively easy method of threading one set of sticks through the other is recommended. The sticks for the garden basket are white, four fourteen inches long and nine nine inches long. the completed bottom twelve inches by seven inches. The nine short sticks are split in their centres and the four long ones threaded through them. The short sticks are then spaced as shown in Diagram 29, the length of stick beyond the pairs at each end being three inches. The slath is tied-in, opened-out with white in a

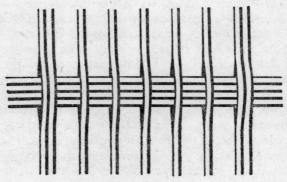

Diagram 29

similar manner to that used in a round bottom, all the sticks being ultimately opened-out into singles, the five sticks that are already single being, of course, left as they are. When a second pair of white rods has been worked out, brown is used for the remainder of bottom. Butts are pieced-in to butts, and tops to tops, and when about half the bottom is completed Reverse Pairing is worked for the remainder, to overcome the strong tendency in an oval bottom to twist. In the reverse pairing, which is like a fitch, the two rods are at the back of the work, and the left-hand rod is brought to the front, passed in front of the next bottom-stick, and put through to the back again, this being repeated with each rod alternately.

The stakes are white, forty-one in number, single

stakes being inserted at the sides of bottom, and two to each of the other stick-ends except one in one end, which has one stake only, to make the odd number necessary in this case because the siding is a slew. For oval baskets an oval hoop is used, and it will be found a good plan to release the end stakes from this after the upsetting, leaving the side stakes in the hoop until some of the siding has been worked. This is because the sides of an oval basket tend to flow out more than its ends. There are three rounds of upsetting, white, the first four-rod begun with butts. The siding is a two-rod slew, brown, the depth under the top wale being three inches, and the inside top dimensions of the basket at this point being fourteen inches by eight inches. After the slewing, one round of three-rod top-waling, white, is put on, and the stakes brought down to form a three-rod-behind-one border. The cross handle has three bows, pushed down by the sides of three adjoining stakes at each side of basket. The centre bow may be tongued at each end and used to secure the handle. The three bows are brought together by means of randing, brown being used, with one white rod to give variety. Both butts and tops of the randing rods used for this purpose are left on inside of handle, and when both sides have been done, the remainder of handle is lapped with white skeins, with one or more skein leaders to form a pattern.

Oval Buff Shopping Basket, Plate 5.—The bottom of this is seven inches by four inches, with four long and eight short bottom-sticks, cut nine inches and six inches long respectively. This basket is proportionately wider than the garden basket, a matter that can readily be determined by the way the bottom-sticks are set out. In this case the distance between the outer pairs of short sticks is roughly one-half the length of bottom, the remaining four short sticks being spaced equally between the two pairs as before. Except that buff is used throughout, this bottom is tied-in, opened-out, and filled in with ordinary and reverse pairing in the same way as that of the garden basket. The stakes number thirty-nine. The upsetting, which is begun with tops, consists of four rounds of three-rod waling, and the siding is a three-rod slew. This is carried to a depth of four inches, with an inside measurement at this depth of nine inches by six inches. After the upsetting, the two middle stakes on each side are treated as one to form bow-marks, two or three stout pieces of rod being placed between to keep them apart after an inch or so of siding has been worked. In the border—in this case a rope border—the left-hand stake of the two is passed by and cut off later. A listed skein cross handle is begun by inserting two or three bows in the bow-marks, the leader rod being tongued at each end and used to secure the handle.

RECTANGULAR WORK

IN the basket trade all rectangular work is known as "square," but it is thought better here to use the term "oblong" for baskets of that shape. As previously mentioned, rectangular work is on the whole more difficult than oval or round work, though parts of the work may be found even easier. Indeed, the baby's basket described below might be made throughout with little if any more difficulty than that encountered in the making of a round basket. This is chiefly because the corners of the baby's basket are not rectangular at all, but rounded, for it is the corners of rectangular baskets that present most difficulty. These have a strong tendency to slant to the left, this being caused by the upsett. During upsetting, therefore, all rectangular corners should be held well over to the right. Another tendency that has to be counteracted is that of the sides to bulge, and yet another that of the stakes to bunch together away from the corners. If, however, the stakes next to the corners are kept right more than half the battle is won. These should be kept well in while the stroke that passes in front of them is worked, and should be kept parallel with the corners. Bulging can be further prevented by putting rod ties across immediately above the upsett, these being cut off when the basket is picked. The hoop can also help in getting a good shape. This should be oval, not rectangular, somewhat less in length and width than the bottom. Corner stakes are released after the upsett. If a rectangular hoop is used, the stakes are liable to collect in its corners instead of keeping in their proper places.

Two kinds of corners are commonly used in rectangular work, those that employ stout corner-sticks and those that do not. The former is recommended for the novice. The other corner, sometimes called a blunt corner, is formed on two stakes, these being closer together than the two corner stakes are when a corner-stick is set between them. The method of using corner-sticks is dealt with a little later, the baby's basket now to be described having neither corner-sticks nor blunt corners, but rounded ones, which, properly speaking, bring it within the category of oval work, as far as its top is concerned. The bottom, however, is a true oblong one, and the sides and ends of basket are to be kept flat as in in all rectangular work.

Oblong Buff Baby's or Work Basket (Plate 3, Diagram 30).— For the bottom of this basket six bottom-sticks twelve inches long will be needed, four of them about the thickness of a lead pencil, and two somewhat thicker for outside-sticks. Diagram 30 shows the sticks in the screw-block, the outside-sticks being seven inches apart. This diagram also shows a device for preventing the outside-sticks from drawing inwards as the randing proceeds. It consists of a wooden cross-piece, nailed to the left-hand outside-stick, and pinned to the right-hand outside-stick with the awl so that the width of the sticks can be adjusted at will. The bottom is made with buff, two feet six inches to three feet long. First, a pair is put on, a procedure not necessary in a lid, which can be begun straight away with randing. The pair is formed by placing a long rod between the left-hand outside-stick and the next one, with about half its length in front and half at the back, the butt end being in front. The other end is then brought round the outside-stick to the front, behind the second stick, and to the front again and pairing is continued until the butt end of the rod rests against the right-hand outside-stick. The butt is then taken round the outside stick, through to the front, in front of the second stick, and to the back, where it is left resting against the third stick. The other part of the rod is then taken through to the back on the left of the outside-stick, brought round the latter, and then used to begin the ordinary randing, backwards and forwards. When a rod has been worked to its top, this is left at the back, and a new butt laid in the next space so that it rests against the same stick, also at the back, or butts can be laid in to butts, and tops to tops. When the bottom is a little short of ten inches long, another pair is worked in the same way as the first, except that the butt, instead of being left against the stick, is pushed through below the last stroke, between the second and third sticks from the right, where the other end of the rod projects to

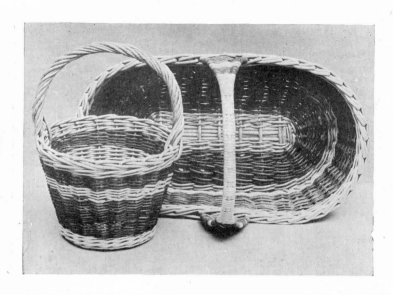

PLATE 5: *Above.*—Round Brown-and-White Blackberry Basket and Oval
Brown-and-White Garden Basket

Below.—Oval Buff Shopping Basket and Willow-edged Tray

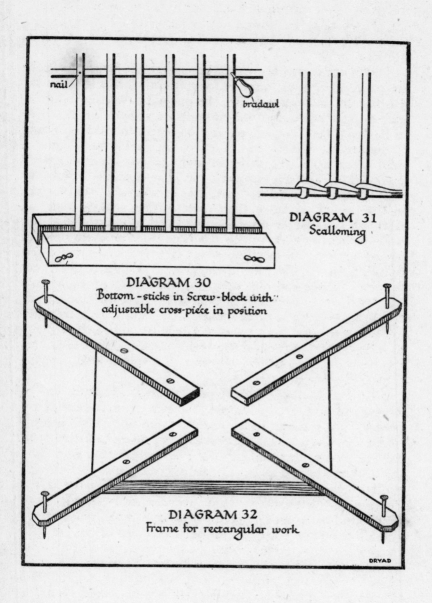

nail

bradawl

DIAGRAM 31
Scalloming

DIAGRAM 30
Bottom-sticks in Screw-block with
adjustable cross-piece in position

DIAGRAM 32
Frame for rectangular work

DRYAD

the front. The bottom is then taken from the block, picked, and the ends of the bottom-sticks cut off close. The cross-piece will previously have been removed when the work got too close to it.

The next process is staking-up, which, as far as the ends are concerned, is the same as for a round or oval basket. In the present basket a stake will be pushed in on the inside of each outside stick, and one on each side of the other stick-ends, less one stake at one end to form an odd number. These are pricked up and gathered into the hoop. For the side stakes, holes are made through the outside-sticks with the bodkin, slanting upwards so that when the stake is pushed in its butt will rest against the second bottom-stick. In the present instance there are thirteen stakes, buff, at each side, the outer ones being placed at a little distance from the corners. After this has been done an extra stake is placed between the existing two at each corner to make the rounded corners introduced into this particular basket. Four rounds of three-rod buff upsetting are now worked, begun with two sets of tops, one at each end. After this the basket is sided to a depth of three inches with buff skeins, the inside top measurements being twelve inches by eight inches. Two rounds of buff three-rod top-waling are then put on, and the basket completed by working the simple plait border previously described.

Close-Randed Buff Picnic Basket (Plate 2, Diagram 32).— This is an advanced example, but can be made easier by having light-randing instead of close-randing. The bottom, which has seven sticks, is twelve inches by eight inches, and this is also the measurement of the basket inside border. The inside depth is four inches. There are fourteen by ten stakes, the corner ones being placed so as to allow for the intro-duction of corner-sticks, which are fixed in position by the first round of upsetting. There are four rounds of upsetting, and after the first has been put on, the corner-sticks are held by the wooden frame shown by Diagram 32. This can be home-made, and can be adjusted by means of the screws to various sizes and proportions of length and width. The centre piece should be at least half an inch thick, but the arms need not be so stout. Each of the latter has a nail at its end which is pushed into top of corner-stick, the latter being cut two or three inches longer than the depth of basket so that the frame will be high enough not to interfere with the work of siding. As will be seen in the illustration, the picnic basket has two rounds of waling and a twisted-rod handle half-way up. There are eight sticks in the lid, which is fastened to basket by two hinges, and secured in front by two staples on border of basket and a rod.

OTHER SHAPES AND KINDS OF WORK

SCALLOMING (Diagram 31).—As the diagram shows, this is the process of fixing the butt of a rod—previously cut to a long slype or tongue—to a stouter rod or stick. This method was used in the Half-Moon Buff Cycle Basket, Plate 4. The curved part of the bottom of this basket is formed by turning a stout rod in the same way as for a handle-bow, a temporary rod tie being placed across the two ends to keep them from springing apart. To the curved part of this hoop rods to serve as both bottom-sticks and stakes for back of basket are scallomed, and after the bottom is made, the stakes for the curved part can also be scallomed. Scalloms are used also for the lids of the "Southport Basket," Plate 3, and in the Boat Basket, on the same page, the handle bows are scallomed to the top framework of basket. Both these baskets are examples of a class of work which may have possibilities of useful development, namely, willow work on frames. By the use of frames, larger baskets, furniture, and other wicker articles are brought within the scope of the fine willow worker. The native willow could be used in the production of the frames, as it already is, for example, in the familiar "stick chair" produced in large quantities in Somerset and other parts of the country.

OTHER DRYAD PUBLICATIONS

CANEWORK

By C. CRAMPTON. Written by a practical basketmaker of many years' experience and recognised as the standard book on the craft, this title includes an introduction to the history of basket making, notes on cane and its uses, hints for the worker on materials, tools and technical terms, and instructions for making numerous articles in cane. viii + 135 pages. Illustrated. Cloth boards.
Net 10s. 6d.

CUT PAPER WORK

By C. RUSSELL COX. Written for teachers of pupils whose ages may range from six years onward, and the various aspects of the work are offered in graded form without, however, imposing a hard-and-fast scheme. One chapter is entirely devoted to the cutting of floral shapes, and others to coloured paperwork in the infant school, co-operative work, picture making, colour, etc. 75 pages. Illustrated in colour, line and half tone. Cloth boards.
Net 10s. 6d.

A HANDWRITING MANUAL

By ALFRED FAIRBANK. Intended to assist teachers to an understanding of the principles of ordinary handwriting: pens, posture, speed, joins, rhythm, spacing, etc., it explains in detail the stages from printscript to a hand satisfying all the requirements of legibility, speed, beauty and health, and presents numerous models written by the author and other contemporary writers or taken from sixteenth-century books and documents. vi + 40 pp. Profusely illustrated. Cloth boards.
Net 5s.

A TEXT-BOOK OF NETTING

By B. ST. G. COLLARD. Gives instructions for plain netting, square-mesh netting, circular netting, fancy pattern netting, with details for making various nets and bags by these methods. A chapter is also included on repairing nets, splicing, whipping, copying a net, etc. viii + 63 pages. Illustrated in half-tone and with numerous diagrams. Paper boards.
Net 5s.

THE DRYAD PRESS, SAINT NICHOLAS ST., LEICESTER.

*This book is a publication of the Dryad Press—sub-
sidiary of Dryad Limited, Leicester, of which Dryad
Handicrafts is another branch. It is one of an extensive
range of books and leaflets dealing with various kinds of
craftwork, all of which are written by experienced crafts-
men and -women. A list of these publications will gladly
be forwarded on request.*

DRYAD LIMITED,
Saint Nicholas St., Leicester.
London Showrooms: 22, Bloomsbury St., W.C.1.